Fabrics & Supplies

For sewing ... needles, thread, pins, thimble, iron, ironing board, basting thread, scissors, pin cushion

For making templates ...

cardboard, graph paper, rubber cement, pencil, ruler, triangle, eraser, protractor, compass, scissors, patchwork templates (comes in handy)

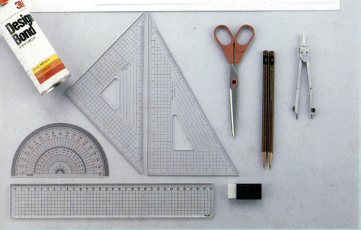

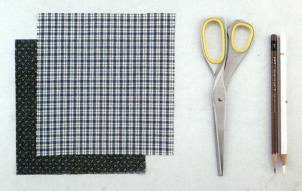

For cutting fabric ...

sandpaper, pencil, scissors

At the Cotton Shop

When it is difficult to make up your mind on what to buy at the fabric shop, decide on something similar to what is on this page. Don't just buy your favorite big prints and striped fabrics but mix one or two solids. Solids, mixed with patterned and striped fabrics create nice patchwork pieces.

When buying fabrics, choose cotton of similiar weight and texture. Lightweight cotton is easier to sew and quilt. Stretchy knits and loosely woven fabrics that ravel easily are not suitable for patchwork.

Wash Fabrics

Separate dark and light color fabrics. Wash three minutes in washing machine and wring dry. Smooth out wrinkles and iron while damp. Now, you are ready to start.

When fabric is new, make sure it is preshrunk and colorfast. Washing takes out excess starch and makes fabric easier to handle.

Fabrics shown on this page are of actual size and were used in the following designs:

A Rail Fence	L Hexagon Star	V Log Cabin,
B Card Trick	M Cube Work	Courthouse Steps
C Kaleidoscope	N Grandmother's Flower Garden	
D Ohio Star	O Mosaic	
E Cherry Basket	P Star and Hexagon	
F Rambler	Q Pointing Star	W Cathedral
G Christian Cross	R Clam Shell	Window
H LeMoyne Star	S Dresden Plate	X Puff
I Virginia Star	T Grandmother's Fan	Y Yo Yo
J Katie's Favorite	U Wedding Ring	
K Old-fashioned Nosegay		

3

The Basics of Patchwork

No.1   Draw designs in actual size

Glue graph paper on cardboard. Draw design in actual size. Measurements are not given for the patterns included in this book, therefore draw designs in desired size and divide into three or four subunits to make basic squares and triangles. Use HB pencil and draw designs accurately using ruler, compass and protractor.

Drawing Kaleidoscope pattern:

Right angles are made by drawing vertical and horizontal lines on graph paper. Therefore, it is easy to draw squares and triangles. Cardboard helps the compass from slipping and therefore, you can draw nice and neat lines.

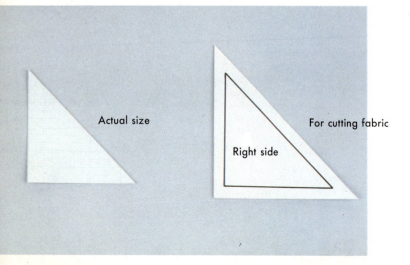

Actual size

For cutting fabric

Right side

No.2   Making Templates

Cut out cardboard designs with sharp scissors to make templates. Lay templates on cardboard. Mark 0.7cm (¼") seam allowance lines with pencil and cut out to make templates including seam allowance. First set of templates is for marking seam lines; second set of templates is for marking cutting lines. Be sure to mark right sides of templates because templates can be flipped over and used on wrong sides. Make two or three extra sets of templates because template edges become dull from repeated use.

Making templates for Cardtrick design:

Make two sets of templates: one for marking seams and one for cutting fabrics. Mark grain lines, fabric color and number of pieces on templates for cutting fabrics.

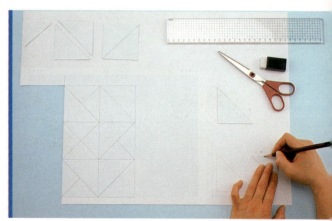

● How to divide into three equal subunits:

When a number can not be divided evenly into three equal subunits, use a ruler. Find a number that is bigger than your measurement and that can be divided evenly by three. Place ruler diagonally as shown in following illustration. 24 ÷ 3 = 8 and so mark 8 and 16. With a right-angled triangle, draw perpendicular lines and you have divided your measurement in three equal subunits. Do the same by finding numbers that are divisible by 4 or 5 when you want to divide into 4 or 5 equal subunits.

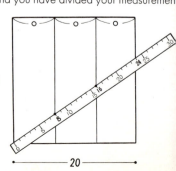

Divide 20cm (8") length into three equal subunits.

No.3 Mark with pencil

Set out sandpaper, HB pencil and templates (one set for cutting fabric and one set for marking seam lines). Prewash fabric and iron. Correct fabric grain.

Sandpaper is a great help when marking. Marking fabrics with pencils can be slippery and tricky. Sandpaper grasps the fabric and lines can be easily drawn. Always use sharp pencils since dull pencils can change the measurement.

Tips on marking with pencil

Pencil marks using templates for cutting fabric.

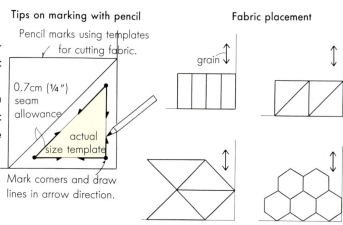

0.7cm (¼") seam allowance

actual size template

Mark corners and draw lines in arrow direction.

Fabric placement

grain

Marking with templates for cutting fabric:

Place fabric right side down on sandpaper (wrong side facing up). Align template with fabric grain and mark with pencil. According to print pattern (print, stripes, checks), place desired print pattern in center of triangle or when aligning stripes, do not mark consecutively. Fabric grain may be changed in order to enhance print pattern. Mark fabrics keeping in mind what kind of image you would like to create.

Marking with templates for seam lines:

After you have marked cutting lines, position templates for marking seam lines in the center. Don't forget to mark matching notches on the inner side of seam allowance.

Marking on dark fabric

It is difficult to cut or sew when lines are not visible. Use white, yellow, red or other coloring pencils.
Be sure to sharpen pencils.

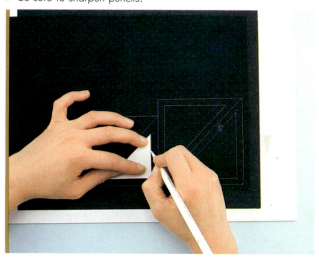

No.4 Cutting fabric

Cut on pencil lines. Lay out pieces and check to see if you have cut the correct fabrics according to pattern design.

When you have laid out the pieces, it will be easier to see which lines you must sew.

Lay out pieces.

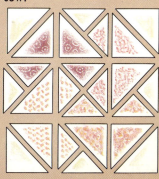

Learn Running Stitch, Backstitching is Important!

Running stitch is the basic sewing stitch for patchwork.
Remember to make a backstitch at the beginning and end.
Patchwork pieces are so small that it is necessary to
backstitch in order to reinforce seams.

1 Pin pieces

With right sides together, match corners and pin perpendicular to seam lines. Pin corners and then pin at regular intervals. Do not leave wide space between pins. When sewing curved seams, match notches and pin at intervals of 0.5 - 1 cm (¼ - ⅜").

2 Running stitch

Cut sewing thread into 30 - 50 cm (12" - 20") length, knot end and sew using thimble. Don't worry if your stitches are not straight or even. Your second piece will be better than your first.

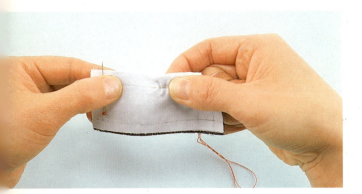

3 Smoothing out stitches

It is very important to pull the thread taut after sewing so that the stitches will stay. Smooth out stitches a couple of times with your left thumb and forefinger and proceed.

4 When smoothing out stitches is done too harshly

When sewing bias seams and you have smoothed out the stitches too harshly, the seams will have stetched and the shape will be distorted (squares become parallelograms). Be careful when smoothing out stitches. Do a few stitches at a time.

A bad example of a stretched seam

5 Iron seam allowance

Ironing is essential for a flat and smooth finish. With right sides together and the seams sewn, iron lightly. Open pieces and iron from wrong side, making sure the seam allowance is pressed to one side. It is easier to iron seam by seam than to iron the whole block after it is pieced.

6 Backstitching

Always backstitch at the beginning and end of seam.

Hold piece upside down and insert needle one stitch from the beginning. At the end of seam, take one backstitch and make knot. This makes it easier when many seams meet at center but the knots will not bunch together.

Sew from mark to mark.

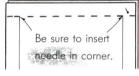

Backstitching at the end

Backstitching where seams overlap

Backstitching at the beginning

When sewing from edge to edge

Sew from mark to mark.

about 1 cm (3/8")
Knot can be made on opposite side.

Sew from edge to edge.

Be sure to insert needle in corner.

Backstitching where seams overlap

When seam allowance is pressed in a certain direction, backstitch at point where seams overlap.

When seam allowance is freestanding, backstitch so that you will not be sewing down seam allowance.

When many seams meet, backstitch before and after the seams overlap.

When sewing one side of triangle or square, always take backstitch at corner and then re-pin other side, continue sewing.

Backstitching where seams overlap

backstitch

Backstitching where many seams overlap

Make one backstitch

Next, sew square

Sew triangle

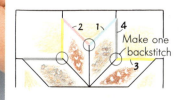

2 1 4
Make one backstitch
3

Understanding the Illustrations

1   Check to see which pieces are to be sewn from mark to mark or from edge to edge.

Sewn from edge to edge

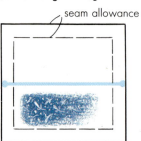

seam allowance

Sewn from mark to mark

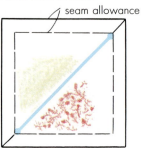

seam allowance

2   Numbers 1 & 2 on page 16 mean that 1 is to be sewn first and then re-pinned, and 2 to be sewn next.

3   Seam allowance is to be pressed in the direction shown in the picture and then trimmed.

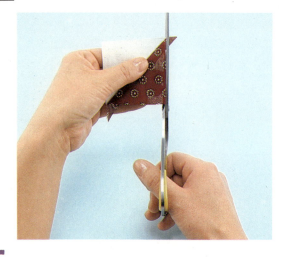

4   Seam allowance is to be pressed according to diagram of wrong side.

5   When referring to diagram of wrong side, some overlaying seam allowances are omitted in order to help understand the direction of underlying seam allowances.

You are now a patchwork expert!

Let's start making different patterns!

RAIL FENCE

Drafting/ Divide finished size in 3 equal subunits. When you have your square, divide the square in thirds so you will have 3 rectangles.

Templates/ Make two sets of templates: one for cutting fabric (add 0.7cm (¼") seam allowance) and one for marking seam lines.

Cutting Fabric/ Mark 3 different fabrics and cut required number of pieces. Arrange pieces according to design.

Piecing/ Read pages 4 through 8 and proceed.

★ Drafting

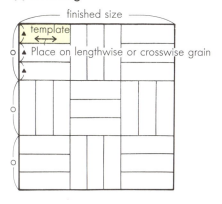

Place on lengthwise or crosswise grain

▮▮ START

Sew from edge to edge and piece into square.

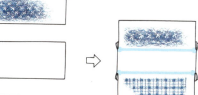

Sew from mark to mark and piece 3 blocks in a row.

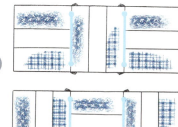

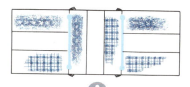

Sew from mark to mark and piece 3 blocks in a row.

▮▮ FINISH

Sew from mark to mark and piece 3 rows into one block.

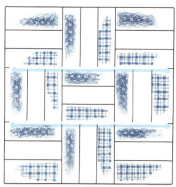

How to press seam allowance (wrong side)

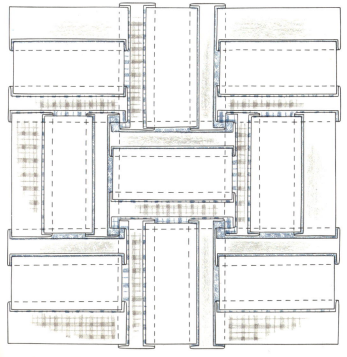

CARD TRICK

Drafting/ Divide finished size into 3 equal subunits. When you have your square, draw diagonal line and make triangle.

Templates/ Make 2 sets of templates for A and B: one for cutting fabrics (0.7cm (¼") seam allowance has been included) and one for marking seam lines.

Cutting Fabric/ Mark 5 different fabrics and cut required number of pieces. Arrange according to design.

Piecing/ Read pages 4 through 8 and proceed.

★ Drafting

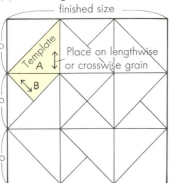

finished size

Template A — Place on lengthwise or crosswise grain

B

//START

Sew from mark to mark; mark to edge and piece into square.

Sew from mark to mark and piece 3 blocks in a row

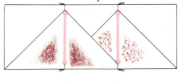
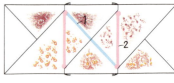
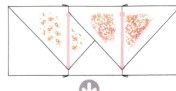

//FINISH

Sew from mark to mark and piece 3 rows into a block.

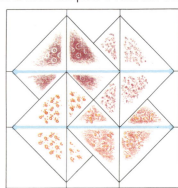

How to press seam allowance (wrong side)

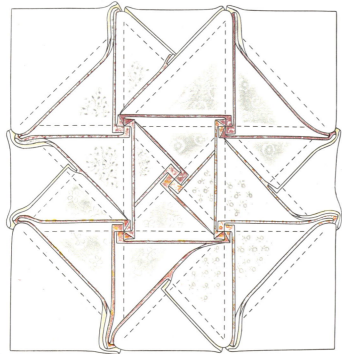

KALEIDOSCOPE

Drafting/ Divide finished size in half. When you have your square, divide square in half. With compass at pink corner, draw circle using the length from pink corner to center of square as the radius. Repeat this at the four pink corners. Connect 8 blue marks to make triangle.

Templates/ Make 2 sets of templates for A and B: one for cutting fabrics (0.7cm (¼″) seam allowance included) and one for marking seams lines. Check fabric grain! Piece B is usually cut on grain as shown in diagram. However, the piece shown in this picture has been cut on bias grain so that the flower is centered in the piece.

Cutting Fabric/ Mark 3 different fabrics and cut required number of pieces. Arrange pieces according to design.

Drafting

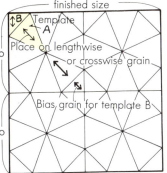
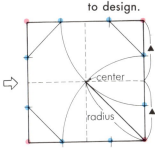

Piecing/ Read pages 4 through 8 and proceed.

How to press seam allowance
(wrong side)

Top layer of seam allowances have been omitted to show how the underlying seams are pressed.

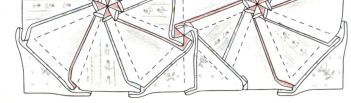

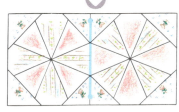

**START**

Sew from mark to mark and piece into square.

Sew from mark to mark and piece into one row.

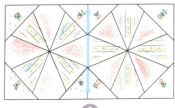

FINISH

Sew from mark to mark and piece 2 rows into one block.

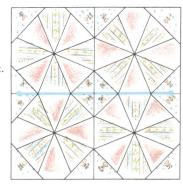

OHIO STAR

Drafting/ Divide finished size into 3 equal subunits. When you have your square, draw diagonal lines to make tri-angles.

Templates/ Make 2 sets of templates for A and B: one for cutting fabrics (0.7cm (¼") seam allowance included) and one for marking seam lines.

Cutting Fabric/ Mark 3 different fabrics and cut required number of pieces. Arrange pieces according to design.

Piecing/ Read pages 4 through 8 and proceed.

★ Drafting

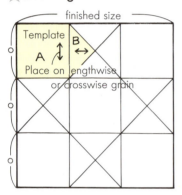

 **START**

Sew from mark to edge, edge to edge and make square.

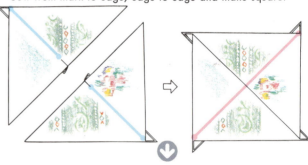

Sew from edge to edge and piece into 3 vertical rows.

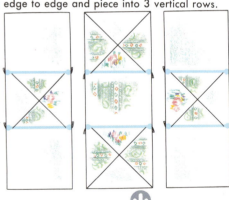

How to press seam allowance (wrong side)

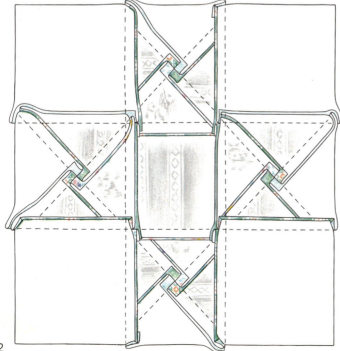

FINISH

Sew from edge to edge and piece 3 rows into one block.

CHERRY BASKET

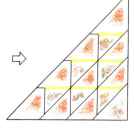

Drafting/ Divide finished size into 5 equal subunits. When you have your square, draw diagonal lines to make triangles A through D and rectangle. For E, use compass on red point and draw half circle.

Templates/ Make 2 sets of templates for A - E: one for cutting fabrics (0.7cm (¼″) seam allowance included) and one for marking seam lines.

Cutting Fabric/ Mark 3 different fabrics and cut the required number of pieces. Arrange pieces according to design. Cut piece E on bias as indicated in diagram. Mark pattern E on right side of fabric piece A to indicate applique placement.   **Piecing/** Read pages 4 through 8 and page 27 and   proceed.

⭐ **Drafting**

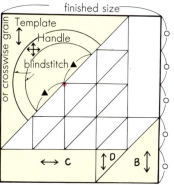

//START

Sew from mark to mark and piece into triangle.

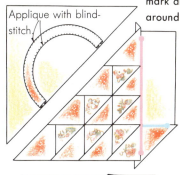

Sew from mark to mark and piece around triangle.

Applique with blind-stitch.

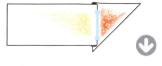

How to press
seam allowance (wrong side)

Top layer of seam allowances has been omitted to show how the underlying seam allowances are pressed.

//FINISH

Sew from mark to mark and piece into square.

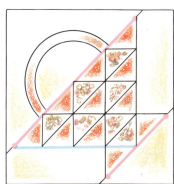

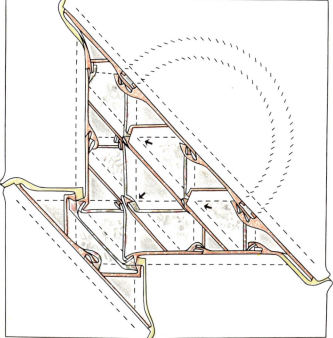

RAMBLER

Drafting/ Divide finished size into 8 equal subunits. Draw diagonal lines to make triangles A through D and square.
Templates/ Make 2 sets of templates for A through D: one for cutting fabrics (0.7cm (¼") seam allowance included) and one for marking seam lines. Check fabric grain! Piece B is usually cut on grain as shown in diagram. However, this piece has been cut on bias grain so that the flower is in the center of the piece.
Cutting Fabric/ Mark 3 different fabrics and cut required number of pieces. Arrange pieces according to design.
Piecing/ Read pages 4 through 8 and proceed.

★ Drafting

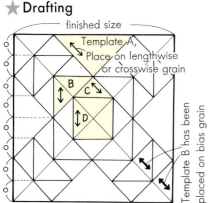

finished size

Template A, Place on lengthwise or crosswise grain

B C D

Template B has been placed on bias grain

Sew from edge to edge and piece into diagonal strip.

START

Sew from edge to edge in order of 1 - 3.

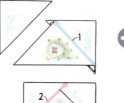

-1

2

3

FINISH

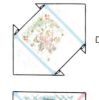

Sew from edge to edge and piece 3 rows into one block.

How to press seam allowance (wrong side)

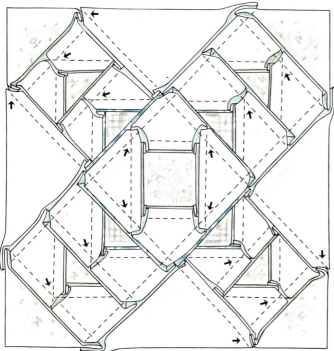

Top layer of seam allowances has been omitted to show underlying seam allowances.

14

CHRISTIAN CROSS

Drafting/ Divide finished size into 8 equal subunits. Draw diagonal lines to make rectangle, square, triangles: A through D.

Templates/ Make 2 sets of templates for A through D: one for cutting fabrics (0.7cm (¼″) seam allowance included) and one for marking seam lines.

Cutting Fabrics/ Mark 3 different fabrics and cut the required number of pieces. Arrange pieces according to design.

Piecing/ Read pages 4 through 8 and proceed.

★ Drafting

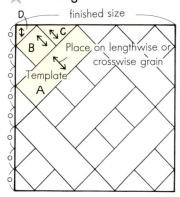

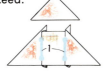

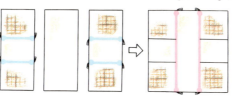

▰▰ START

Sew from edge to edge, mark to mark in the order of 1 and 2.

Sew from mark to mark diagonally in 3 strips in the order of through 3.

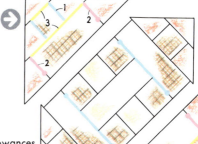

Top layer of seam allowances has been omitted to show the underlying seam allowances.

▰▰ FINISH

Sew from mark to mark and piece 3 rows into one block.

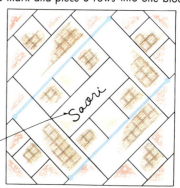

Backstitch with 4 strands of embroidery floss. (Refer to P.48)

How to press seam allowance (wrong side)

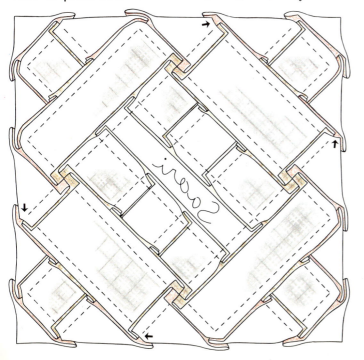

LEMOYNE STAR

Drafting/ Divide finished size in half. Using a compass, draw 4 circles using length from pink corner to center of square as the radius. Connect 8 blue marks to make square. Draw rhombus and triangle using length of square.

Templates/ Make 2 sets of templates A through C: one for cutting fabrics (0.7cm (¼″) seam allowance included) and one for marking seam lines.

Cutting Fabrics/ Mark 3 different fabrics and cut required number of pieces. Arrange according to design.

Piecing/ Read pages 4 through 8 and proceed.

★ **Drafting**

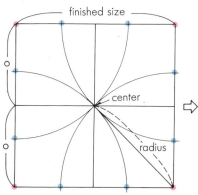
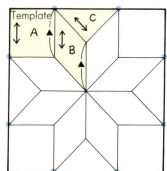

How to press seam allowance
(wrong side)

Top layer of seam allowances has been omitted to show the underlying seam allowances.

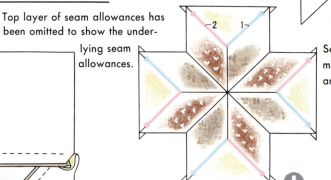

▰ START

Sew from mark to mark and piece into star shape.

Sew from mark to mark in the order of 1 and 2.

▰ FINISH

Sew from mark to mark in the order of 1 and 2.

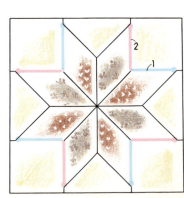

VIRGINIA STAR

Drafting/ Decide on size and measurements as you did for LeMoyne Star on P.16. Divide rhombus into quarters.
Templates/ Make 2 sets of templates for A through C: one for cutting fabrics (0.7cm (¼″) seam allowance included) and one for marking seam lines.
Cutting Fabrics/ Mark 5 differents fabrics and cut the required number of pieces. Arrange pieces according to design.
Piecing/ Read pages 4 through 8 and proceed.

★ Drafting

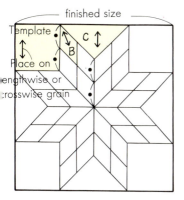

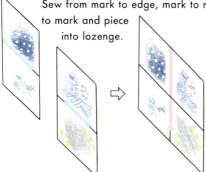

START
Sew from mark to edge, mark to mark, edge to mark and piece into lozenge.

Sew from mark to mark and piece into star shape.

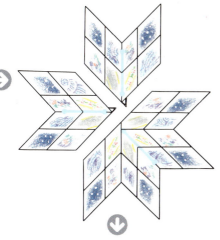

How to press seam allowance
(wrong side)

Top layer of seam allowances has been omitted to show the under-lying seam allowances.

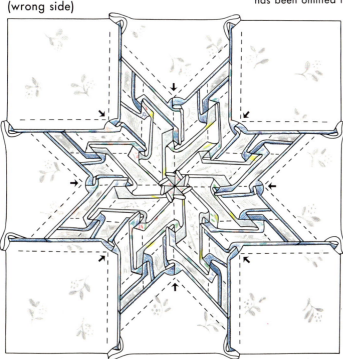

FINISH
Sew from mark to mark in the order of 1 through 4.

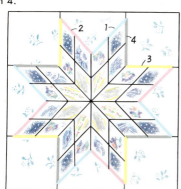

KATIE'S FAVORITE

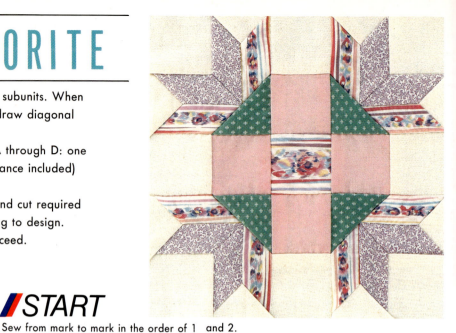

Drafting/ Divide finished size into 5 equal subunits. When you have the center square and triangle, draw diagonal lines to make rhombus and triangle.

Templates/ Make 2 sets of templates for A through D: one for cutting fabrics (0.7cm (¼") seam allowance included) and one for marking seam lines.

Cutting Fabrics/ Mark 5 different fabrics and cut required number of pieces. Arrange pieces according to design.

Piecing/ Read pages 4 through 8 and proceed.

★ Drafting

finished size

Template
A ↕
Place on lengthwise or crosswise grain
B ↔ C
D ↔ ↔

//START

Sew from mark to mark in the order of 1 and 2.

Sew from mark to mark and make 3 horizontal rows.

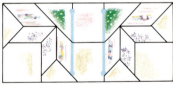

//FINISH

Sew from mark to mark and piece 3 rows into one block

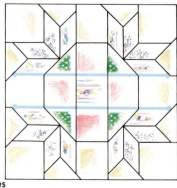

How to press seam allowance

(wrong side)

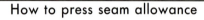
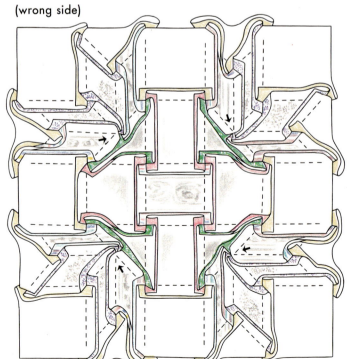

➡ Top layer of seam allowances has been omitted to show underlying seam allowances.

OLD-FASHIONED NOSEGAY

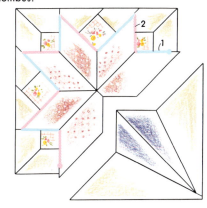

Drafting/ Divide finished size into 4 equal subunits. Draw diagonal lines to make pieces A through G.

Templates/ Make 2 sets of templates for A through G: one for cutting fabrics (0.7cm (¼″) seam allowance included) and one for marking seam lines. Mark templates A through C and A′ through C′ so that right and wrong sides are distinguishable.

Cutting Fabrics/ Mark 5 different fabrics. A through C should be placed symmetrically and on the same grain. Cut the required number of pieces for A through G. Arrange the pieces according to design.

Piecing/ Read pages 4 through 8 and proceed.

★Drafting

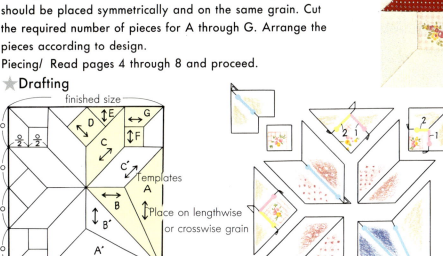

▊START

Sew from mark to mark in the order of 1 and 2.

Sew from mark to mark and sew around rhombus.

How to press seam allowance (wrong side)

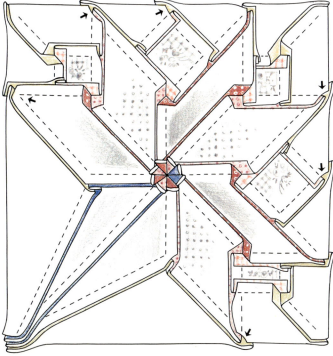

▊FINISH

Sew from mark to mark in the order of 1 and 2.

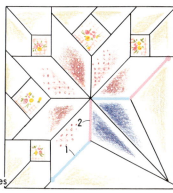

➡Top layer of seam allowances has been omitted to show underlying seam allowances.

Paper-liner Method

Paper-liner method requires a paper template for each fabric piece and each piece is then, carefully whip-stitched together.

In this case, all the seams are open. Paper templates are needed for each piece, however, since all the seam allowances are open, there is no complication in which direction the seams should be pressed.

Use lightweight cardboard, the thickness of a postcard, for templates.

You will need basting thread!

The patterns given on the following pages 20 through 25 were made using the paper-liner method.

When piecing patterns with running stitch, sew from mark to mark and press seam allowances in one direction as shown on p.22 in the Cube Work design.

HEXAGON STAR

Drafting/ Bisect finished size of hexagon. Using 1/2 length of finished size as the radius, draw circle. Using the same radius, draw an arc that intersects the circle. Continue around the circle, making a total of six marks. Connect these marks consecutively to form the hexagon. Draw diagonal lines to make triangles and rhombuses.

Templates/ Make 2 sets of templates: one for cutting fabrics (0.7cm (¼″) seam allowance included) and one for marking seam lines.

Cutting Fabrics/ Mark 4 different fabrics and cut required number of pieces. Arrange according to design.

Piecing/ Read pages 4 through 8 and page 21 and proceed.

Seam allowance (wrong side)

Press seam allowances at center in one direction so that it forms a windmill. Press from right side. Cut basting and remove paper templates.

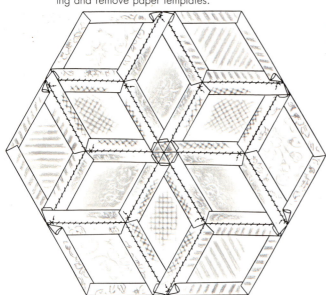

★ **Drafting**

finished size

center

template

Place on lengthwise or crosswise grain

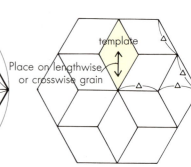

START

Whipstitch in the order of 1 and 2.

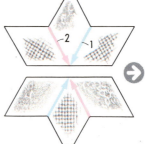

FINISH

Whipstitch in the order of 1 and 2.

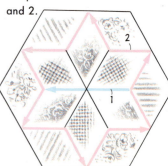

✚ Basting

Press seam allowances. Baste paper template and fabric piece making sure that they do not slip.

1. Place template on wrong side of fabric piece. Press seam allowance.

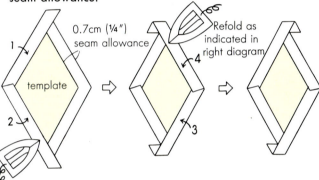

1
2
0.7cm (¼")
seam allowance
template
4
3
Refold as indicated in right diagram

2. Basting center rhombuses.

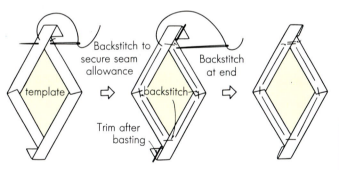

Backstitch to secure seam allowance
template
backstitch
Backstitch at end
Trim after basting

3. Basting other rhombuses.

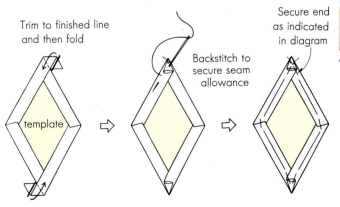

Trim to finished line and then fold
template
Backstitch to secure seam allowance
Secure end as indicated in diagram

✚ Whipstitch

With right sides together, whipstitch 2 pieces by inserting the needle at the edge of fabric piece. Use single strand of matching thread.

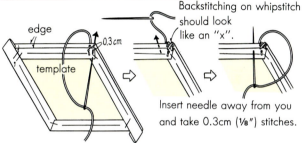

edge
template
0.3cm
Backstitching on whipstitch should look like an "x".
Insert needle away from you and take 0.3cm (⅛") stitches.

Insert needle 0.3cm (⅛") from corner and pull thread. Insert needle into corner and again into the first stitch.

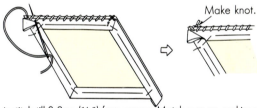

Make knot.

Whipstitch till 0.3cm (⅛") from corner. Match corners and insert needle. Again insert needle in previous stitch.

✚ Whipstitching Corners

For the center, insert needle in corner, pull thread 1½ around center as shown in diagram and continue whipstitch.

For the center where 3 pieces meet, whipstitch each 2 pieces at corner as shown in diagram.

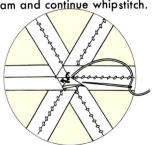

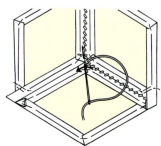

CUBE WORK

Drafting/ Divide finished size in 6 equal subunits. Use ⅙ of finished size as the radius and draw circle. Draw hexagon using circle. (Refer to p.20) Connect marks and center to make rhombuses.

Templates/ Make 2 sets of templates: one for cutting fabrics (0.7cm (¼″) seam allowance included) and one for marking seam lines.

Cutting Fabrics/ Mark 3 different fabrics and cut required number of pieces. Arrange according to design.

Piecing/ Read pages 4 through 8 and proceed.

How to press seam allowance (wrong side)

➡ Top layer of seam allowances has been omitted to show underlying seam allowances.

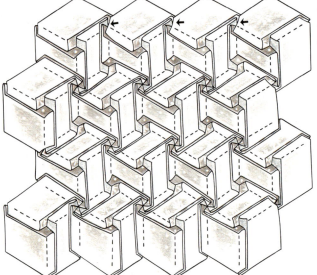

GRAND MOTHER'S FLOWER GARDEN

Drafting/ Divide finished size into 8 equal subunits. Draw hexagon using ⅛ of finished size as the radius. (Refer to p.20.)

Templates/ Make 2 sets of templates: one for cutting fabrics (0.7cm (¼″) seam allowance included) and one for marking seam lines.

Cutting Fabrics/ Mark 3 different fabrics and cut required number of pieces. Arrange according to design.

Piecing/ Read pages 4 through 8 and page 21 and proceed.

★ Drafting

finished size

template

Place on lengthwise or crosswise grain

START

Sew from mark to mark in the order of 1 and 2 to make hexagon.

Sew from mark to mark and piece 4 in a row.

FINISH

Sew from mark to mark in the order of 1 and 2 and piece 4 rows to make one block.

★ Drafting

template

Place on lengthwise
or crosswise grain

finished size

//START //FINISH

Whipstitch starting from center hexagons in
the order of 1 through 4.

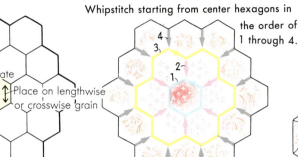

4
3
2
1

Seam allowance (wrong side)

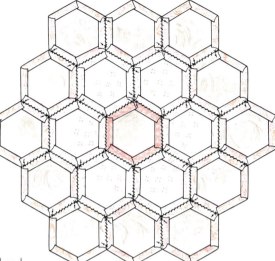

✚ Basting

Place paper template on wrong side of fabric piece
and press seam allowance. Baste.

Refold seam allowance as shown in diagram.

Backstitch at beginning and end.

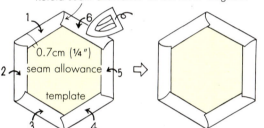

1
6
0.7cm (¼″)
seam allowance
2
5
template
3
4

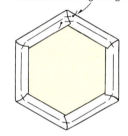

✚ Whipstitch

When you can not hold pieces right sides
together, hold pieces as shown in picture and
whipstitch towards center.

M O S A I C

Drafting/ Divide finished size into 17 equal subunits and
draw hexagon using 1/17 of finished size as the radius.
(Refer to p.20.)

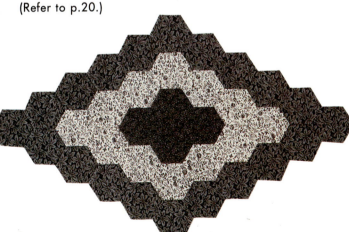

Templates/ Make 2 sets of templates: one for cutting
fabrics (0.7cm (¼″) seam allowance included) and one for
marking seam lines.
Cutting Fabrics/ Mark 3 different fabrics and cut required
number of pieces. Arrange according to design.
Piecing/ Read pages 4 through 8 and page 21 and
proceed.

finished size

★ Drafting

template

Place on lengthwise
or crosswise grain

//START

Whipstitch 4 center
hexagons.

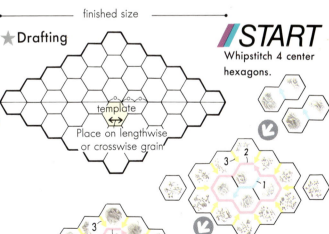

3
2
1

Whipstitch in the ord-
er of 1 through 3.

3
2
4
1
1
4

//FINISH

Whipstitch in the ord-
er of 1 through 4.

STAR AND HEXAGON

Drafting/ Divide finished size into 4 equal subunits and draw hexagon using ¼ of finished size as the radius.

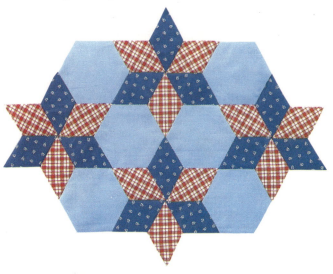

★ Drafting

Place on lengthwise or crosswise grain.

Template A

B

finished size

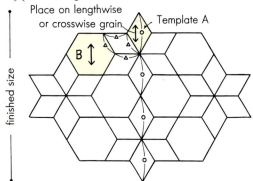

Seam allowance

(wrong side)

Remove basting and press as shown in diagram.

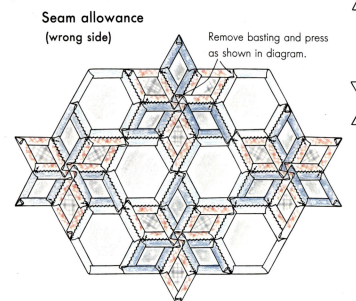

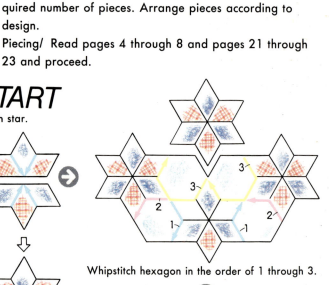

Draw rhombuses using previous hexagon. (Refer to p.20.) Draw hexagon with sides in the same measurement as one side of rhombus.

Templates/ Make 2 sets of templates for A and B: one for cutting fabrics (0.7cm (¼") seam allowance included) and one for marking seam lines.

Cutting Fabrics/ Mark 3 different fabrics and cut required number of pieces. Arrange pieces according to design.

Piecing/ Read pages 4 through 8 and pages 21 through 23 and proceed.

▌START

Whipstitch star.

Whipstitch hexagon in the order of 1 through 3.

▌FINISH

Whipstitch in the order of 1 and 2.

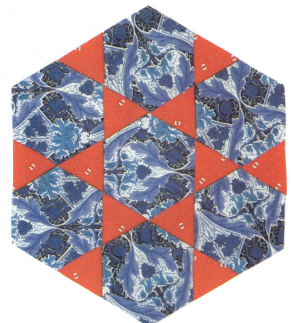

Piecing/ Read pages 4 through 8 and pages 21 through 23 and proceed.

Drafting/ Divide finished size into 6 equal subunits. Draw hexagon using ⅙ of finished size as the radius. (Refer to p.20.) Draw triangle by dividing hexagon into 6 subunits.

Templates/ Make 2 sets of templates for A and B: one for cutting fabrics (0.7cm (¼″) seam allowance included) and one for marking seam allowance.

Cutting Fabrics/ Mark 2 different fabrics and cut required number of pieces. Arrange according to design.

★Drafting

✚ Basting

Place paper template on wrong side of fabric piece and press. Baste.

1. Basting center triangle:

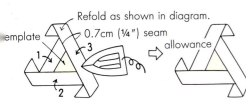

Refold as shown in diagram.
0.7cm (¼″) seam allowance
Backstitch at beginning and end.

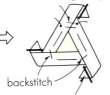

backstitch
Trim after basting.

2. Basting other triangles:

Trim to finished line and fold.   Backstitch at beginning and end.

Secure as shown in diagram.

Backstitch at corners.

// START

Whipstitch triangles and hexagons in the order of 1 and 2.

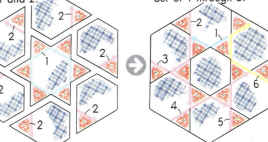

// FINISH

Whipstitch in the order of 1 through 6.

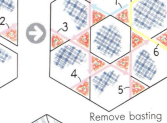

Remove basting and press as shown in diagram.

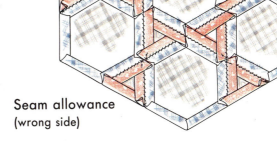

Seam allowance (wrong side)

Applique

Applique is the technique by which fabric pieces cut into template shapes are applied to a background fabric with a blindstitch. Ironing helps to make neat applique projects.

CLAM SHELL

Drafting/ Divide finished size into 6 equal subunits and draw squares. Draw circles around pink marks.

Templates/ Make 2 sets of templates: one for cutting fabrics (0.7cm (¼″) seam allowance included) and one for marking seam lines.

Cutting Fabrics/ 1 Background fabric. Mark 5 different fabrics (you need pieces at top edge) and cut required number of pieces. Arrange pieces according to design.

Piecing/ Read pages 4 through 8 and proceed.

★ Drafting

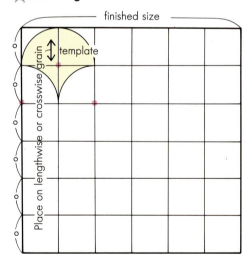

finished size

template

Place on lengthwise or crosswise grain

//FINISH

Draw squares on background fabric. Place clam shells on background fabric, baste and blindstitch.

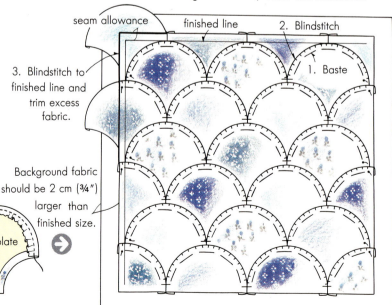

seam allowance

finished line

2. Blindstitch

3. Blindstitch to finished line and trim excess fabric.

1. Baste

Background fabric should be 2 cm (¾″) larger than finished size.

//START

Sew running stitch as shown in diagram. Place template and make clam shell shape.

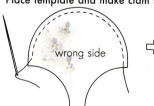

wrong side

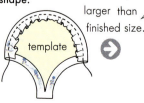

template

✚ Pressing seam allowance

Press seam allowances with the tip of iron.

✚ Blindstitch

Use single strand of matching thread.

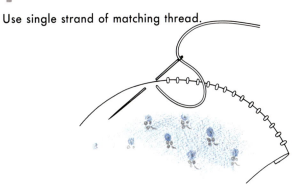

Blindstitching the handle of Cherry Basket

✚ With iron, press into shape of handle.

Cut notches and fold seam allowance. Press. (Be sure not to stretch bias section.)

✚ Appliqueing handle.

Mark handle E on fabric piece A with pencil. Place handle piece on mark and baste. Blindstitch from inner side.

DRESDEN PLATE

Drafting/ Bisect finished size and draw circle with ½ finished size radius. Draw small circle with radius of ¹⁄₁₀ or ³⁄₂₀ and another circle with radius of ¼ of previous circle. Using a protractor, divide the circle into 16 parts. Draw lines. Draw curved or pointed spokes on outside edge.

Templates/ Make 2 sets of templates for A and B: one for cutting fabrics (0.7cm (¼") seam allowance included) and one for marking seam lines.

Cutting Fabrics/ 1 Background fabric. Mark 9 different fabrics and cut required number of pieces. Arrange according to design.

★ Drafting

Piecing/ Read pages 4 through 8 and page 27 and proceed.

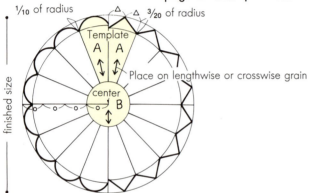

1/10 of radius   3/20 of radius

Template A A

Place on lengthwise or crosswise grain

center B

finished size

Fold background fabric into quarters. Iron the folds into the fabric. Place the plate on applique background, using the ironed folds as guidelines for centering. Baste and applique.

START

Sew in the order of 1 through 3 and make circle.

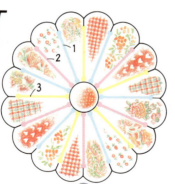

FINISH

Curved seams

Do running stitch in middle of seam allowance. Place template and pull thread. Press to secure shape.

Template

Pointed seams

Fold seam allowance as shown in diagram to make pointed spoke. Continue around the outside edge and press.

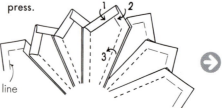

Seam line

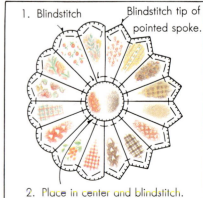

1. Blindstitch   Blindstitch tip of pointed spoke.

2. Place in center and blindstitch.

GRANDMOTHER'S FAN

Drafting/ Divide finished size into 20 equal subunits.

Draw $^{6.5}/_{20}$ and $^{12.5}/_{20}$ circles as shown in diagram. Using protractor, divide into 6 equal parts.

Templates/ Make 2 sets of templates for A through C: one for cutting fabrics (0.7cm (¼″) seam allowance included) and one for marking seam lines. Mark matching notches on actual size templates.

Cutting Fabrics/ Mark 8 different fabrics and cut required number of pieces. Arrange according to design.

Piecing/ Read pages 4 through 8 and proceed.

★ Drafting

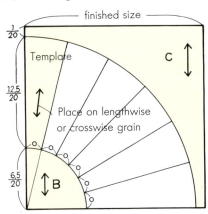

How to press seam allowance
(wrong side)

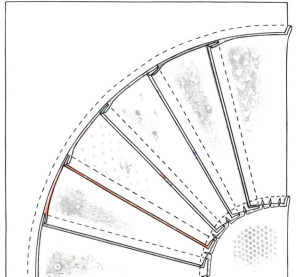

//START

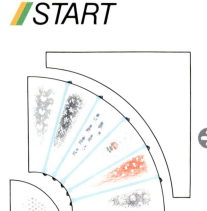

Sew from edge to edge and piece into fan.

//FINISH

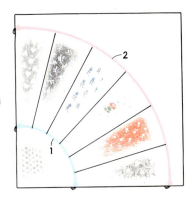

Sew from edge to edge in the order of 1 and 2.

Piecing Curved Seams

Match notches and pin closely.
Cut notches in seam allowance and sew tiny stitches.

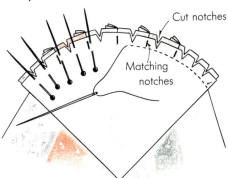

WEDDING RING

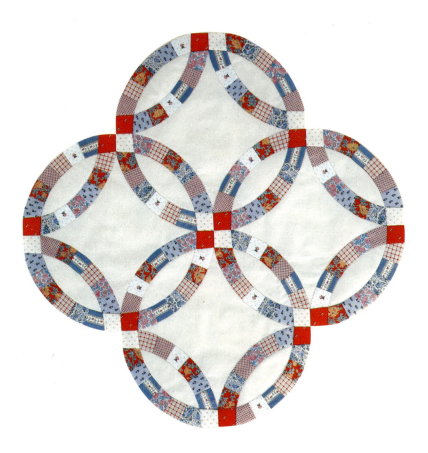

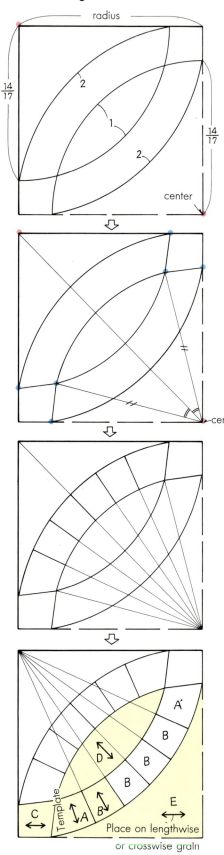

Drafting/ In order to draft a quarter of Wedding Ring (=double arc), choose a measurement for the diameter. Draw square in the length of the radius. Choose width of band. Draw circle 1 and 2 as shown in top diagram. Connect blue marks and pink mark as shown in second diagram. Divide into 6 equal parts as shown in third diagram. Make templates A through E.

Templates/ Make 2 sets of templates for A through E: one for cutting fabrics (0.7cm (¼″) seam allowance included) and one for marking seam lines. For template E, mark one piece from the template, then flip it on its vertical axis and mark the second and so on until you have come back to the first piece. Mark matching notches on templates A, B and D, E. For template A′, use wrong side of template A.

Cutting Fabrics/ Mark 11 different fabrics and cut required number of pieces. Arrange according to design.

Piecing/ Read pages 4 through 8 and proceed.

START

Sew from mark to mark and piece A through C.

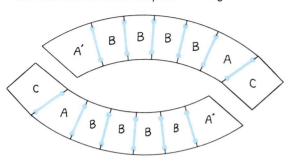

Sew from mark to mark and piece into double arc.
(Place A - C on D, matching notches.)

FINISH

Sew from mark to mark in the order of 1 and 2.

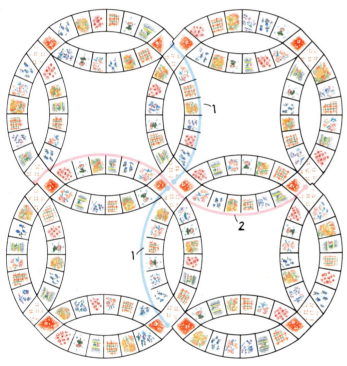

Sew from mark to mark in the order of 1 and 2.

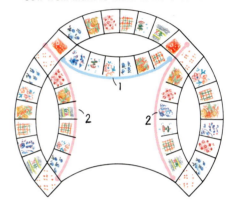

How to press seam allowance (wrong side)

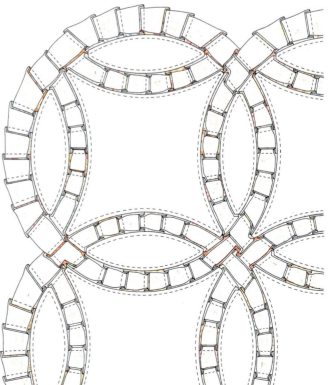

LOG CABIN

Check to see if one rectangle is the same length as the square or if all the rectangles are of the same length. Piecing differs depending on the formation.

Use batting and lining allowing the Log Cabin to be quilted as it is pieced. This saves quilting time for the beginner.

Drafting/ Choose size for one Log Cabin block. Divide square into 12 square subunits. The 4 square subunit center is square A. Draw rectangles around square A.

Templates/ Make 2 sets of templates for A: one for cutting fabrics (0.7cm (¼") seam allowance included) and one for marking seam lines. Template B is used to check to see if the Log Cabin pattern is constructed in a square, so make B in actual size.

Cutting Fabrics/ Cut required number of batting and lining in finished size and add 1cm (⅜") seam allowance. Mark right side of fabric piece A and cut required number of pieces. For the remaining 10 colors, add 1.4cm (½") seam allowance and cut long strips of required length. Mark each strip.

★ Drafting

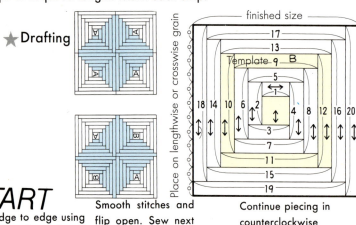

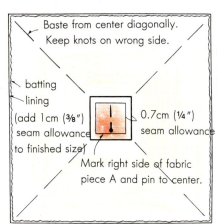

Baste from center diagonally. Keep knots on wrong side.

batting
lining
(add 1cm (⅜") seam allowance to finished size)

0.7cm (¼") seam allowance

Mark right side of fabric piece A and pin to center.

Piecing the blocks

▟START

Sew from edge to edge using running stitch and sew through all 4 layers. Trim before sewing.

Smooth stitches and flip open. Sew next piece.

Continue piecing in counterclockwise direction.

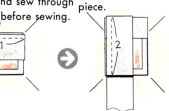

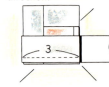

1. Sew right sides together.
With right sides together, pin and sew from mark to mark.

2. Trim batting.
Fold seam allowance, overlap batting slightly and trim.

Straight Furrow

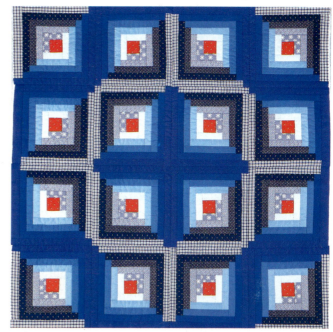

Barn Raising

Variations

Four blocks of design A (1 & 2 dark color, 3 & 4 light color) will look like top diagram on p.32. Four blocks of design B (1 & 2 light color, 3 & 4 dark color) will look like bottom diagram on p.32. Look out for the corners where the blocks are pieced. In design A, there are two rows of the same color. In Straight Furrow in the left diagram, same number of A and B blocks are arranged so that there are dark and light lines running diagonally. In Barn Raising, block A is arranged symmetrically. Variations can be made by arranging the same blocks in different positions.

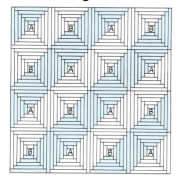

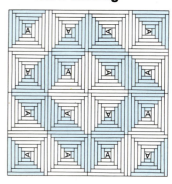

//FINISH

Sew to piece 12. Place template B and adjust shape so it is a full square. Mark and continue sewing till piece 17.

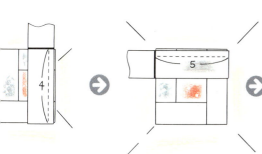

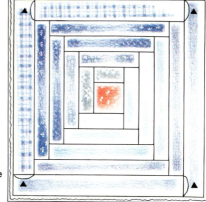

From pieces 18 to 20, sew only the strips where marked with ▲.

3. Whipstitch batting.
With single strand of thread, whip stitch.

4. Blindstitch lining.
Fold lining, pin and blindstitch.

5. After you have pieced all the blocks, quilt in the ditch (running stitch along seams) with matching thread.

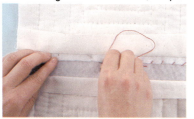

LOG CABIN

Compare this with Barn Raising on the previous page. This Log Cabin was pieced without batting and lining. All the rectangles around the square are of the same size. Watch out when you sew No.5.

Drafting/ Choose a measurement for one square block. Divide block into 12 equal subunits. The center four subunits is piece A. Draw rectangles around piece A.
Templates/ Make 2 sets of templates for A through F: one for cutting fabrics (0.7cm (¼″) seam allowance included) and one for marking seam lines.
Cutting Fabrics/ Mark 11 different fabrics and cut required number of pieces. Arrange according to design.

▮▮START

Sew from mark to edge.

Smooth stitches. Flip open strip and sew next piece edge to edge.

Sew from edge to edge.

Fold No.1 and sew to edge.

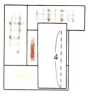

Sew No.5 section.

★ Drafting

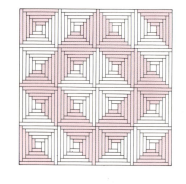

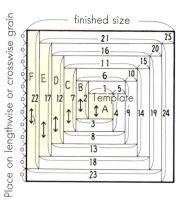

Place on lengthwise or crosswise grain

finished size

▮▮FINISH

Lay out 16 blocks and piece together by sewing from mark to mark.

Sew from mark to edge and piece remaining strips counterclockwise.

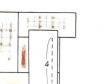
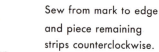
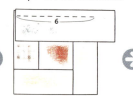

COURTHOUSE STEPS

Drafting/ Choose a measurement for one square block. Divide block into 23 equal subunits. The 6 center subunits is piece A. Draw rectangles around piece A.

Templates/ Make 2 sets of templates for A through G: one for cutting fabrics (0.7cm (¼") seam allowance included) and one for marking seam lines.

Cutting Fabrics/ Mark 7 different fabrics and cut required number of pieces. Arrange pieces to construct block.

START

Sew from edge to edge.

Smooth stitches. Flip open and sew next piece edge to edge.

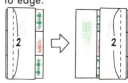

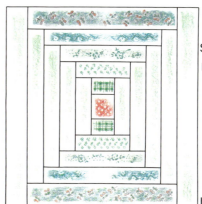

Sew top & bottom, left & right pieces. Sew from edge to edge.

FINISH

Lay out 9 blocks and piece together by sewing from mark to mark.

★ Drafting

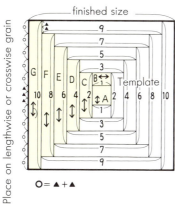

Place on lengthwise or crosswise grain

finished size

O = ▲ + ▲

How to press seam allowance (wrong side)

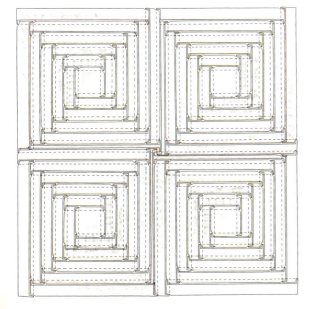

How to press seam allowance (wrong side)

CATHEDRAL WINDOWS

Drafting/ Divide finished size into 3 equal subunits. Double the length of one subunit and draw square using that measurement. This will be the background piece. Draw diagonal lines as shown in the drafting diagram. Draw square 0.2cm (1/16″) smaller than the square marked with △. This will be the window pane piece.

Templates/ Make 2 templates for background piece: one for marking fabrics (1cm (3/8″) seam allowance included) and one for marking seam lines. Make 1 template in actual size for window pane piece.

1. Baste background fabric

1cm (3/8″) seam allowance

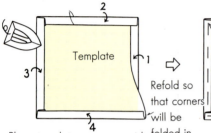

Place template on wrong side of background fabric, fold seam allowance and press. Remove template.

Keep knots on right side.

Refold so that corners will be folded in the same direction.

Make sure square is not distorted when basting. Always insert needle at corner to secure shape. (wrong side)

Use single strand of basting thread and baste through center of seam allowance.

Picture showing basting procedure.

Template

1. Fold the 4 corners towards the center. Secure with pin and sew center with single strand of matching thread. Press lightly and remove basting.

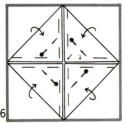

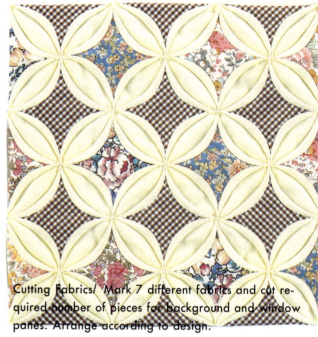

Cutting Fabrics/ Mark 7 different fabrics and cut required number of pieces for background and window panes. Arrange according to design.

★ **Drafting**

finished size

background fabric   9 pieces

Place on lengthwise or crosswise grain

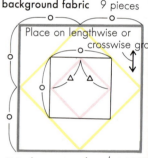

Window pane piece (no seam allowance)

12 plaids, 12 prints

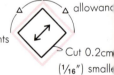

Cut 0.2cm (1/16″) smaller than original square

2. Folding procedures

Fold background fabric and iron on center fold.

Match corners and fold background fabric diagonally. Press the folds into the fabric. Do the same for the other direction. Be sure you do not smooth out other crease.

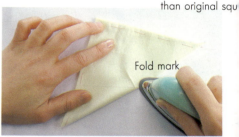

Fold mark

2. Turn the square over so that a smooth piece of fabric is facing you. Fold the 4 corners to the center. Sew center, press lightly and remove basting.

How to sew center (1): follow diagram. Insert needle diagonally from front to back following numbers 1 - 5, 6 - 10.

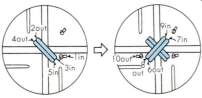

How to sew center (2): follow numbers and insert needle from the back through to front between folds and secure by stitching in a cross. Cut thread.

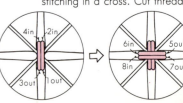

3. Joining the squares

Finishing wrong side: roughly whipstitch edge of squares.

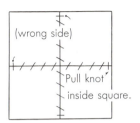

(wrong side)

Pull knot inside square.

Whipstitching background squares

With right sides together, whipstitch background squares. Be sure to backstitch at beginning and end. (Refer to p.21.) Join squares in horizontal rows. Join rows. When piecing large projects like bedspreads, backstitch back and forth.

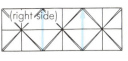
(right side)

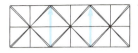

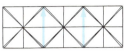

4. Inserting the window pane

Blindstitch window pane piece.

Use single strand of thread matching window pane fabric. Place window pane piece on background square and blindstitch (refer to p.27). Start blindstitch from edge and make sure knots are not visible.

● Secure corners: secure corners of background squares. Pull needle from between folds and sew diagonally. Leave knot on wrong side.

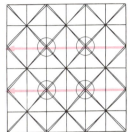

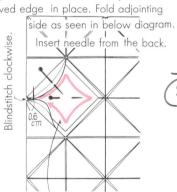

1

Fold the edge of the background diamond in a smooth curve over the pane. Pin the curved edge in place. Fold adjointing side as seen in below diagram. Insert needle from the back.

Blindstitch clockwise.

0.6 cm

Check color coordination of window pane pieces.

2

Secure corners of first and fourth curve by stitching only the curve layers.

0.6 cm

3

After securing corners, insert needle exactly at the corner stitch and pull needle 0.4cm (⅛") from corner (this secures corner in place).

0.4 cm

4

Blindstitch curve and leave backing free. (At corners, stitch only curve layers.)

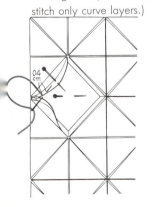

0.4 cm

5

Make knot on back.

All 4 corners should be sewn securely 0.6cm (¼") from edge.

0.6 cm

0.6cm

● Finishing edges

Place window pane pieces (12) in the triangular pieces. Blindstitch 2 curves and fold and baste remaining part to the back.

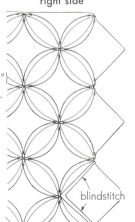

right side

blindstitch

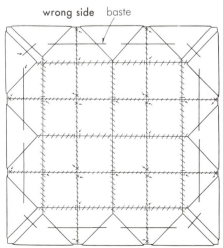

wrong side   baste

P U F F

Drafting/ Choose a measurement for 1 puff. This will be the size of the backing. Divide this measurement into 7 equal parts and mark the place and number of pleats. Draft puff tops.

Templates/ Make 2 sets of templates for backing and puff tops: one for cutting fabrics (0.7cm (¼″) seam allowance included) and one for marking seam lines. Mark center and pleats position.

Cutting Fabrics/ Mark backing and puff tops on right side. Cut required number of pieces in 4 different fabrics. Arrange according to design.

Drafting

finished size

$\frac{1}{7}$ backing

Mark center

$\frac{1}{7}$

▲ = Placement of pleats

Place on lengthwise or crosswise grain

● = $\frac{1}{7}$

puff top

● = width of pleats

▌START

Place top fabric square against backing fabric square and fold excess fabric into a pleat.

Pin at corner and center.

top fabric (right side)

backing

0.7cm (¼″) seam allowance

Baste; backstitch at pleats.

Sew from edge to edge and sew in horizontal row.

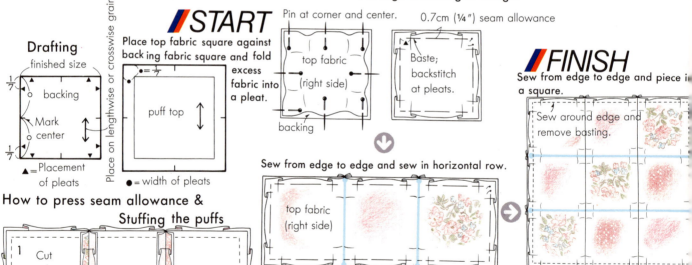

top fabric (right side)

▌FINISH

Sew from edge to edge and piece in a square.

Sew around edge and remove basting.

How to press seam allowance & Stuffing the puffs

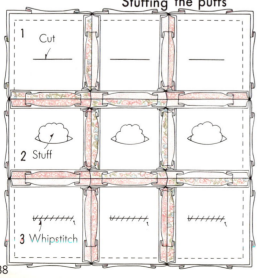

1 Cut

2 Stuff

3 Whipstitch

Stuffing the puff:
Snip the backing at the center of each square and insert stuffing with hands.

Whipstitch:
Using single strand of thread matching backing fabric, stitch closings with whipstitching.

Y O   Y O

Drafting/ Divide finished size into 4 equal subunits. Draw circle with a diameter in ¼ of the measurement.
Templates/ Make 2 sets of templates: one for cutting fabrics (0.7cm (¼") seam allowance included) and one for seam lines.
Cutting Fabrics/ Mark 16 different fabrics and cut required number of pieces. Arrange pieces according to design.

Drafting

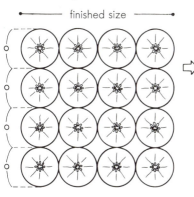

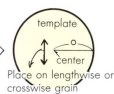

finished size

template
center
Place on lengthwise or crosswise grain

o = radius of finished Yo Yo

//START

Use single strand of matching thread. Fold seam allowance. Leave 2cm at end and do a running stitch 0.2cm from edge and 0.8 - 1cm apart. Leave 2 cm (¾") at end and cut thread.

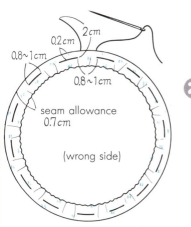

2cm
0.2cm
0.8~1cm
0.8~1cm
seam allowance 0.7cm
(wrong side)

Pull thread and gather. Tie ends.

Pull 2 ends of thread so that running stitch comes to center. Pull again and knot ends twice. Cut thread so it will not show. Make required number of Yo Yo.

//FINISH

Arrange finished Yo Yo in order. With wrong sides together, stitch. Keep adding more horizontally. Then join row. In order to make a neat Yo Yo project, always keep the center aligned.

Joining the Yo Yo

Join by backstitching the edge of Yo Yo.

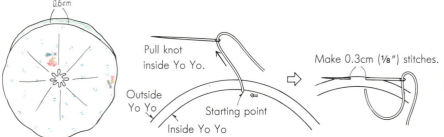

0.6cm

Pull knot inside Yo Yo.

Outside Yo Yo
Starting point
Inside Yo Yo

Make 0.3cm (⅛") stitches.

Do a backstitch.

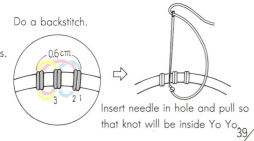

0.6cm

3 2 1

Insert needle in hole and pull so that knot will be inside Yo Yo.

Enjoying Quilting

After you have finished the top, let us start to
quilt. Layer the top with batting and lining and
start sewing. Don't worry about your stitches!

What you need:
Pieced top, batting (cotton stuffing is O.K.), lining (prewashed
lightweight cotton fabric), quilting thread, basting thread, needles,
pins, scissors (dressmaker shears), scissors (for cutting thread), thimble (for both left and right hand), ruler, pencils, ballpoint pens,
eraser, dressmaker's carbon, cellophane (for drawing quilting lines
and designs), quilting frame (would be convenient)

Drawing Quilting Lines

Press seam allowances from wrong side for a flat and smooth finish.

+ Using a ruler

To draw straight lines, use a ruler and draw with HB pencil.

+ Using dressmaker's carbon

1. Choose design size and position.
2. Make template for piece with quilting design. Trace template on paper.
3. Draw quilting design on paper with template shape.
4. Place paper with quilting design (3) on pieced top. Adjust position and pin.
5. Insert dressmaker's carbon between top and quilting design. Place cellophane on top. Trace design with ballpoint pen.

Basting

Basting is necessary to secure the pieced top, batting and backing layers. Baste vertically, horizontally and diagonally and around the edge. Baste in straight lines or in curved lines but do not baste too closely or else the quilting lines will disappear. Roll basted project so that there will not be any creases from folding. Quilting takes time!

+ Basting in straight lines

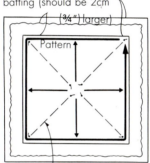

lining (should be approximately 1cm (⅜") larger than batting)
batting (should be 2cm (¾") larger)
Pattern

Smaller projects can be basted in straight lines from the center.

+ Basting in curved lines

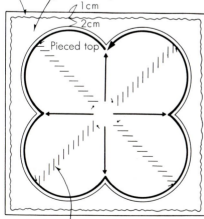

Trim lining and batting to finished size.
1cm
2cm
Pieced top

For large projects, baste diagonally from center.

Quilting

✚ Up-down Method

This is the needlepoint method where you push the needle down with the right hand and return it from underneath with the left hand. This is time-consuming but assures even stitches.

Beginning of quilting

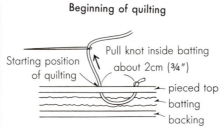

Starting position of quilting
Pull knot inside batting about 2cm (¾")
pieced top
batting
backing

End of quilting

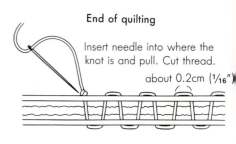

Insert needle into where the knot is and pull. Cut thread.

about 0.2cm (¹⁄₁₆")

Quilting Lines

Choose your favorite quilting line. Make sure you are quilting all 3 layers evenly. Learn to finish off edge.

✚ Quilting Vertically and Horizontally

On the Rail Fence pattern, quilting was done vertically and horizontally. Quilting right next to seams is called "quilting in the ditch".

✚ Quilting Diagonally

Diagonal quilting was done on the Kaleidoscope pattern.

Finishing edge with piping

With right sides together, sew piping and quilted project. Attach piping to all 4 sides. Backstitch at corners.

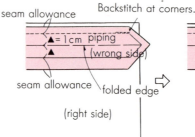

seam allowance
▲ = 1cm piping (wrong side)
seam allowance folded edge
(right side)

With right sides together, sew corners. Fold seam allowance and turn inside out.

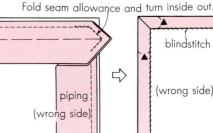

piping (wrong side)
blindstitch
(wrong side)

Finishing edge with piping

With right sides together, machinestitch.

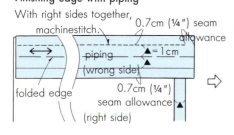

0.7cm (¼") seam allowance
▲ = 1cm
piping (wrong side)
folded edge
0.7cm (¼") seam allowance
(right side)

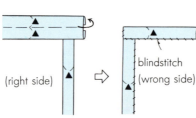

(right side)
blindstitch (wrong side)

✚ Quilting Stitch

Quilt as you would do a running stitch. Take 2 or 3 stitches. It is difficult to have the same even stitches on the top and back. Wear a thimble on your left middle finger and check to see that the needle goes through all 3 layers. In large projects, keep left hand under quilt. For beginners, start with the Up-down Method and when you have become used to quilting, proceed with the running stitch. Practice using the quilting frame.

✚ Quilting Designs

A flower design was quilted in the Wedding Ring.

✚ Quilting Along Seams

The LeMoyne Star was quilted 0.4cm (⅛″) from seams. When drawing quilting lines, trim 0.4cm (⅛″) off actual size template and trace.

Blindstitch Backing

Trim backing 1cm (⅜″) larger than pieced top.

Trim batting to actual size.

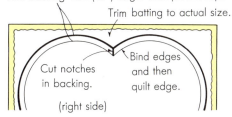

Cut notches in backing.

Bind edges and then quilt edge.

(right side)

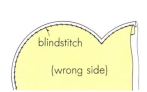

blindstitch

(wrong side)

Binding with Backing

folded edge 0.7cm (¼″) seam allowance

Trim

0.7cm (¼″) seam allowance of pieced top

(right side)

0.5cm

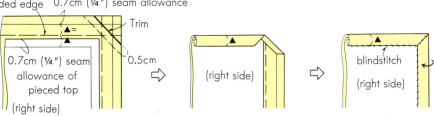

(right side)

blindstitch

(right side)

Cushion

Directions on p.48

POWDER ROOM

Bag

Materials

Fabric .... Polka dot broadcloth 90cm x 65cm (36"x26")
Unbleached muslin .... 58cm x 61cm (23⅛" x 24⅜")
Printed fabrics (2 kinds) ... 48cm x 27cm (19⅛" x 10¾") each
Lightweight batting .... 90cm x 110cm (36" x 44")

Cut 4 batting in the size of 45cm x 48cm (18" x 19⅛"). Trim excess batting after quilting front and back piece.

Drafting
Front & Back

Cut fabric with seam allowance given in ( ) where designated. Add 1cm (⅜") seam allowance to all other pieces.

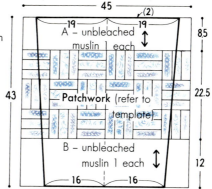

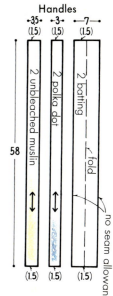

Handles

Directions

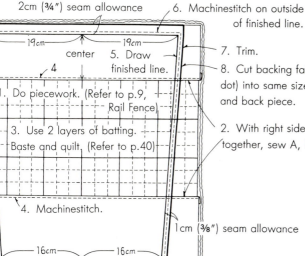

2cm (¾") seam allowance

6. Machinestitch on outside of finished line.

center   5. Draw finished line.

7. Trim.

8. Cut backing fabric (polka dot) into same size as front and back piece.

1. Do piecework. (Refer to p.9, Rail Fence)

3. Use 2 layers of batting. Baste and quilt. (Refer to p.40)

2. With right sides together, sew A, B.

4. Machinestitch.

1cm (⅜") seam allowance

Template (actual size)

Add 0.7cm (¼") seam allowance and cut fabrics.

36 each of polka dot, flower print and printed fabric.

12. With wrong sides together, insert lining bag. Blindstitch top edge. Secure lining with a half-backstitch.

9. Make handles and attach to front and back of bag.

Machinestitch twice.

2cm (¾") seam allowance

finished line

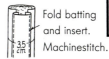

Fold batting and insert. Machinestitch.

10. With right sides together, sew front and back; and lining. Sew sides and bottom.

11. Make gusset.

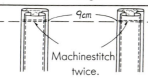

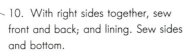

Sew seam allowance to batting.

Secure gusset

bottom

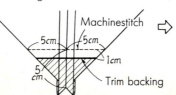

Machinestitch

Trim backing

Materials

Fabrics — unbleached muslin
75cm x 95cm (30″ x 38″)
dark printed fabric 23cm x
26cm (9⅛″ x 10⅜″)
white printed fabric 30cm
x 15cm (12″ x 6″)
light color printed fabric
13cm x 13cm (5⅛″ x 5⅛″)
#25 Burgandy color embroi-
dery floss
Lightweight batting 50 cm x
100cm (18″ x 36″)
40cm (16″) Zipper
45cm x 45cm (18″ x 18″)
nude cushion

Front side. Add seam allowance given in ( ). After piecing A, measure and cut 1cm (⅜″) from outer edge. Cut 2 layers of batting in the size of Quilt parallel to pieced design.

Cushion/Christian Cross

Directions

1. Piece front side. (Refer to p.15.)
2. Blindstitch 1 on unbleached muslin A.
3. Use 2 layers of batting. Layer pieced front and batting. Baste and quilt (refer to p.40). Embroider.
4. Machinestitch seam allowance of front side.
5. Apply zipper to back side.
6. With right sides together, sew front and back sides. Turn inside out from zipper opening.

50cm x 50cm (20″ x 20″) Trim batting into size of front sides after quilting.

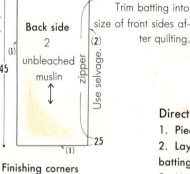

Front side piecework (refer to template)

45 — 8.5 — 8.5 — 28 — 28 — Mariko
Backstitch with 6 1cm (⅜″) strands of embroidery thread.

unbleached muslin A
1cm (⅜″) seam allowance

22.5 (1)
Back side 2 unbleached muslin 45 zipper Use selvage.
2.5 (2) 25 (1)

Backstitch

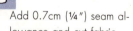

Finishing corners

Cut notches in seam allowance and fold towards inside. Blindstitch.

Template (actual size)

Add 0.7cm (¼″) seam allowance and cut fabric.

Cushion/Kaleidoscope

Materials

Fabrics — Black & white gingham plaids 90cm x 53cm
(36″ x 21⅛″)
Polka dot, print fabric 45cm x 45cm (18″ x 18″) each
Lightweight batting 56cm x 112cm (22⅜″ x 44¾″)
45cm (18″) zipper
50cm x 50cm (20″ x 20″) nude cushion

Add seam allowance given in ( ).
Piece front side. (Refer to template.)

Front side. Cut 2 batting in size of 56cm x 56cm (22⅜″ x 22⅜″)
Trim excess batting after quilting front side.

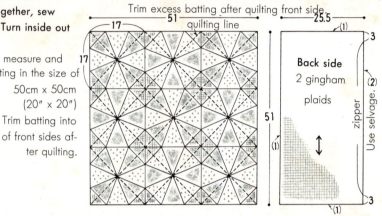

51 — 17 — 17 quilting line
25.5 (1) 3
Back side 2 gingham plaids 51 zipper Use selvage.
(2) (1) 3 (1)

Directions

1. Piece front side. (Refer to p.11.)
2. Layer pieced front with 2 layers of batting. Baste and quilt. (Refer to p.40.)
3. Machinestitch seam allowance of front side.
4. Apply zipper.
5. With right sides together, sew front and back sides and turn inside out from zipper opening.

Applying zipper

1cm (⅜″) 3cm seam allowance

With right sides together 4cm each at bottom and top of zipper.
2. Insert zipper under back side and baste.
3. Machinestitch from right side and remove basting.
4cm

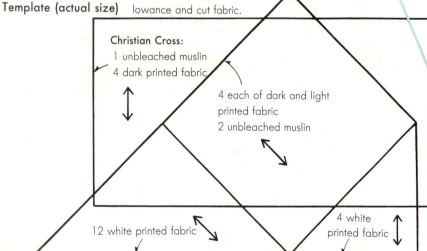

Christian Cross:
1 unbleached muslin
4 dark printed fabric

4 each of dark and light printed fabric
2 unbleached muslin

36 each of polka dot and printed fabric

12 white printed fabric

4 white printed fabric

Kaleidos

36 gingham plaids